IN LOVING MEMORY OF ANGELINA AND MICHAEL BOSCAINO.—B.G.

FOR MY LOVING FAMILY WHOSE FAITH IN ME MADE ALL THINGS POSSIBLE.—R.V.N.

Copyright © 1992 Rabbit Ears Productions, Inc., Rowayton, Connecticut.
Rabbit Ears Books is an imprint of Rabbit Ears Productions.
Published by Picture Book Studio, Saxonville, Massachusetts.
Distributed in the United States by Simon & Schuster, New York, New York.
Distributed in Canada by Vanwell Publishing, St. Catharines, Ontario.
All rights reserved.
Printed in Hong Kong.
2 4 6 8 10 9 7 5 3 1

Library of Congress Cataloging-in-Publication Data
Gleeson, Brian.
The Savior is born / written by Brian Gleeson ; illustrated by Robert Van Nutt.
p. cm.
Summary: A retelling of the events surrounding the birth of Jesus Christ.
ISBN 0-88708-284-X (bk. & cassette) : $19.95. — ISBN 0-88708-283-1 (bk.) : $14.95
1. Jesus Christ—Nativity—Juvenile literature. 2. Bible stories, English—N.T. Gospels.
[1. Jesus Christ—Nativity. 2. Bible stories—N.T.] I. Van Nutt, Robert, ill. II. Title.
BT315.2.G54   1992
232.92′1—dc20   92-4577
CIP
AC

THE SAVIOR IS BORN

WRITTEN BY BRIAN GLEESON ✧ ILLUSTRATED BY ROBERT VAN NUTT

RABBIT EARS BOOKS

Two thousand years ago, in a small village called Nazareth, in the part of Israel known as Galilee, there lived a maiden named Mary.

She was a poor, simple, young woman, but her love of God was strong and pure. She always praised God's greatness and thanked him for what little she had. Her circumstances may have been humble, but her faith in God was unending.

For many years, God had told the people of Israel, through the words of the prophets, that someday he would send a child of peace who would lead them to the kingdom of heaven. This child, they said, would be the one anointed by the spirit of God and was to be the king and Savior of the entire world.

Isaiah, one of those prophets, foretold his coming: "The glory of God shall be revealed; And all people shall see it together; For the mouth of God has spoken it…Behold, a maiden shall bring forth a son, whom she shall call Emmanuel, which means God is with us."

Many people remembered the words of the prophets, and waited anxiously for God to fulfill his ancient promise that would deliver them from their suffering and forgive the sins of the world. The people expected that God would tell them in some way when the child was to be born. But God was silent about his intentions.

One day, as Mary prayed in her home, a bright light suddenly filled the room. She looked up to see the angel Gabriel.

"Rejoice! O favored one," said Gabriel. "The Lord God is with you."

Mary was frightened and trembled in the presence of the angel.

"Do not be afraid, Mary," said Gabriel. "God is pleased with you!"

"Behold! You shall give birth to a son—the Messiah, the world's Savior—and you must name him Jesus. He will be a great king, and his kingdom will have no end."

"But how can this be?" said Mary. "I am only a simple girl of Nazareth. How can I give birth to a great king? It is impossible."

"Nothing is impossible with God," said the angel. "The Holy Spirit will come upon you and cause the child to be conceived. The child will be called the Son of God."

Mary bowed her head, because she now understood that Gabriel was telling her the will of God. She was overwhelmed with happiness that God had chosen her to be the mother of the Messiah, the anointed one. Tears welled in her eyes. How could it be that of all the women in the world, God had picked her?

"I live to serve the Lord," said Mary, lifting her head to look at the angel. "Let it be as you have said."

Gabriel was gone as suddenly as he had arrived.

ary was awestruck, but her heart was filled with joy when she pondered what the angel had said. She had to tell someone what had happened to her. So she got up and quickly began walking into the hills where her cousin Elizabeth lived.

Elizabeth was an older woman who had grieved for most of her life because she was unable to have a child. And she, too, was a good woman, who lived by the word of God. Now, to her surprise, she was going to have a baby. It was a miracle and Elizabeth praised God.

When she came to the gate of Elizabeth's house, Mary called out: "Elizabeth, I have good news to tell you."

When Elizabeth heard the voice, all at once the child in her womb jumped and kicked, and Elizabeth laughed aloud. She knew, before Mary uttered another word, what she had come to tell her.

Elizabeth was suddenly out of breath, but nevertheless, she hurried outside to greet Mary.

"Blessed are you among women," cried Elizabeth. "And blessed is the fruit of your womb. You are to be the mother of my Lord. I was sure of it the moment your greeting reached my ear and the child in my womb leaped for joy."

The two women embraced lovingly. Mary could not contain her happiness and joyously she sang: *"My heart exults in the Lord, for he has looked upon me, his lowly servant. Holy is his name, his love reaches from age to age. He has come to the help of Israel, for he has remembered his promise of mercy."*

Then Elizabeth spoke: "My child is a miracle, but this child of yours will be the Lord and Savior of us all!"

Mary stayed at Elizabeth's home for three months. During that time, the two women kept secret the coming birth of the holy child.

Mary had been promised to a carpenter named Joseph, and it was time to begin their life together. He was to be her husband. So Mary left Elizabeth to be with Joseph.

When Mary came to Joseph, he was distressed to learn that she was already with child. Mary hadn't told him of the angel's visit and that it was the Messiah she carried.

Joseph cared deeply for Mary, but after giving the matter much thought, he decided to break off their betrothal privately. He wanted to spare Mary any public embarrassment, because he was an honorable man and wished her no ill will.

That night, as he lay sleeping, the angel of the Lord appeared to him in a dream.

"Joseph!" said the angel. "Do not be afraid to marry this young woman, for the child she carries is from God. You must name the child Jesus, because he is to be the Savior who leads all to God."

When Joseph woke, he obeyed God's will—though he didn't completely understand it. He married Mary and cared for her tenderly and the child grew within her month by month.

Although Israel had once been a great kingdom, stronger nations had conquered it again and again. And now Israel was under the power of the mighty empire of Rome, whose armies marched victoriously over much of the world.

Now it happened that a decree went out from Caesar Augustus, the emperor of Rome, that all the world should be taxed. Every man in Israel was required to go to the town of his birth to be counted.

Mary was now heavy with child and the difficult trip might endanger her and the unborn baby. But Joseph and Mary had faith in God's plan for them. So they set out for the place of Joseph's birth, the village of Bethlehem.

Their journey was long and hard. Down from the highlands of Galilee they traveled, along the valley of the River Jordan, then up the steep hills past the city of Jerusalem, until at last they came to Bethlehem.

Many travelers streamed into Bethlehem that night as Mary and Joseph entered the gates of the town. When they sought warmth and comfort in the inn, they were told there was no room. Joseph couldn't believe this news. They had traveled for so long and they were so very tired. How could it be that there wasn't a room with a bed for them in all of Bethlehem? Mary needed a place to lie down and rest. They asked everywhere. But the answer was always the same.

At last they came to a humble stable where they could take shelter for the night. At least in the stable there was straw to rest upon and enough warmth from the animals that quietly breathed all around them.

And so it was that Mary gave birth to the child, her son, there in the stable. Then Mary carefully wrapped the child in swaddling clothes and laid him in a manger. She named the child Jesus, as the angel Gabriel had told her.

That night there were shepherds in the fields close to Bethlehem, taking turns looking after their flocks. As they sat around their fire, a great light brightened the sky and the angel of the Lord appeared.

The angel said to them: "Do not be afraid, for behold, I bring you good tidings of great joy for all people. For this night in Bethlehem a child is born. He is the Messiah, the Lord. He lies wrapped in swaddling clothes in a humble manger. Go to him, for he is your true king and the promised Savior of the world."

And suddenly there was a great gathering of angels in the sky singing: *"Glory to God in the highest heaven; Peace on earth to all people of good will."*

When the angels left, the night was again silent. Only the stars shone in the sky. The shepherds looked at one another in astonishment. For so many years before them the people had waited for a Savior.

"Did we dream this?" said one. "We're just poor shepherds. How could it be that the Lord has blessed us with this news?"

"Let us go to Bethlehem and see the child whose birth the Lord has made known to us," said another.

So the shepherds hurried to the town and found Mary and Joseph, and the baby. They looked at him lying in the manger, and they knew.

"It is God's holy child," said one shepherd.

"The angel appeared to us," said another shepherd to Joseph. "He told us that he is the Messiah."

"Yes, it's true, I saw it myself," said the third shepherd. "The sky opened up and there was a great, beautiful light, and a host of angels singing his praise. I can tell this child will be our shepherd."

Joseph remembered the angel of the Lord who came to him in the dream. "I have seen and heard the most miraculous things," he thought to himself.

Mary treasured all the things the shepherds said and pondered them in her heart.

When daylight came the shepherds went through the town of Bethlehem on their way to their flocks, proclaiming the glory of God and the birth of the Messiah to all who would listen.

ar, far away from Bethlehem, in a land in the East, three wise men—Gaspar, Melchior and Balthazar—studied the stars. They believed the stars told of signs from God. On the night that Jesus was born, the wise men saw a new star in the sky.

"What can this star mean?" said Gaspar.

"It is an omen," said Melchior. "It means something very, very important."

"I believe a king has been born who comes to the people of Israel," said Balthazar. "He carries God's message. We must find him."

Day after day they traveled: through the valley of the Tigris and the Euphrates rivers; over the sands of the hot scorching desert; past Damascus and along the River Jordan. At last they came to Jerusalem in the region known as Judea, where Herod was king.

They approached the gates of Herod's palace and asked to see the king. The wise men were shown in and presented to Herod.

"Tell us," said Melchior. "Where is the new king who has just been born?"

"King? What new king?" said Herod. "I am the king, and I know of no other. I assure you that no new king has just been born."

"A new star appeared in the heavens," said Gaspar. "It is a sign from God that the promised king and Savior has been born."

"What do you mean?" Herod shouted. "A new star? A new king?"

"Yes, it is a child from God who is born," said Balthazar. "We have come to give thanks and worship him."

Herod was filled with jealousy and fear. If it were true that another king was born, then it would mean that Herod would have to take measures to preserve his power from this rival.

erod called for the learned men of his court who were familiar with the words of the prophets.

"Who is this king they speak of?" demanded Herod.

One of the court's most distinguished scholars stepped forward to speak.

"It has been told by the prophets that God himself would send a king to Israel," said the scholar. "And that he would be born in Bethlehem. It's quite true what the wise men say!"

Herod was taken aback by the scholar's words. He would have to do something about this new king. Herod dismissed his advisors and addressed the wise men to better plan his treachery.

"Tell me," said Herod. "on what date did you see this star?"

They told him the date.

"Very good," said Herod. "Go and search diligently for the young child at Bethlehem. And when you have found him, bring me word again so that I, too, may come and worship him."

he wise men rejoiced because they now knew where to find the child. When they left the palace, there above them in the sky was the star they had seen rising in the East. They followed the star to Bethlehem until it stopped over the place where the child was.

The sight of the star over the stable filled them with joy. Dressed in their finery and jewels and their cloaks of silk, the wise men stepped down from their camels. They entered the stable and saw Mary and the baby Jesus.

The wise men were overcome instantly with wonder; a great peace filled their souls. They fell to their knees to worship him. Then, opening the treasures they had brought, they offered him gifts of gold and frankincense and myrrh.

"Truly we have found the anointed one of God," proclaimed Balthazar. "His glory and love shall save the people of the world."

The wise men stayed with Jesus for several days to pay homage to him and praise the work of God.

One night, the angel of the Lord came to them in a dream and said: "Do not go back to Herod. He plans evil things for this child and he will use you as his instruments."

The next morning the wise men left Mary, Joseph and Jesus. Heeding the words of the angel, they returned to their country by another way.

Weeks passed and King Herod grew more and more furious. The wise men never returned to tell him where they found the baby Jesus. It was clear to Herod that they had deceived him.

King Herod didn't want to worship Jesus; he wanted to do away with him. He knew the baby was still very young, because the wise men had told him the date when they first saw the star. So he called the commander of his soldiers and gave him this order:

"Go now to Bethlehem and kill every male child who is under two years of age. None must be spared. This new king will be destroyed."

That night in Bethlehem, the angel of the Lord appeared in a dream to Joseph.

"Arise, Joseph," said the angel. "Take the young child and his mother and flee into Egypt. Stay there until I bring you word to return. Herod intends to search for the child and kill him. Go now, Joseph!"

Joseph got up immediately, and taking Jesus and Mary with him, fled that night along the road to Egypt.

The next morning, Herod's soldiers came to Bethlehem and filled the streets with terror. They broke through doors and seized all the young boys of the town. The townspeople pleaded and fought to protect the lives of their children.

But it was no use. Herod's soldiers were merciless. When they marched away they left slaughter in their wake and the weeping of mothers and fathers. Bethlehem had become a town of sorrow.

But Joseph had brought Mary and the child safely into Egypt. They stayed there for some time until the angel of the Lord again appeared to Joseph.

"Herod is dead," said the angel. "The child is safe, for those who wanted to kill him are no more. Take the child and his mother back to your homeland."

So Joseph journeyed back to Israel with Mary and Jesus and took them to Galilee to settle once again in the tiny village of Nazareth.

When they arrived safely in Nazareth they gave thanks to God, for his loving hand had protected them. As Mary and Joseph knelt they were overcome with peace and wonder because God had chosen them as his special servants. God had entrusted to them the child who would one day be called his divine Son. The glory of the Lord shone upon them.

The will of the Almighty was served: This child, the baby Jesus, fulfilled the divine promise God had made long ago to the people of Israel. Jesus would bring the word of God to the entire world and lead his people to the kingdom of heaven.

Mary and Joseph rejoiced in God's love and mercy.

Thus the Savior was born unto the world.